D1053646

Drug Abuse and Teens

Other titles in the *Hot Issues* series

Cult Awareness

A Hot Issue

ISBN 0-7660-1196-8

Date Rape

A Hot Issue

ISBN 0-7660-1198-4

Eating Disorders

A Hot Issue

ISBN 0-7660-1336-7

Sexually Transmitted Diseases

A Hot Issue

ISBN 0-7660-1192-5

Stalking

A Hot Issue

ISBN 0-7660-1364-2

Teens, Depression, and the Blues

A Hot Issue

ISBN 0-7660-1369-3

Teens and Pregnancy

A Hot Issue

ISBN 0-7660-1365-0

The Women's Movement and Young Women Today

A Hot Issue

ISBN 0-7660-1200-X

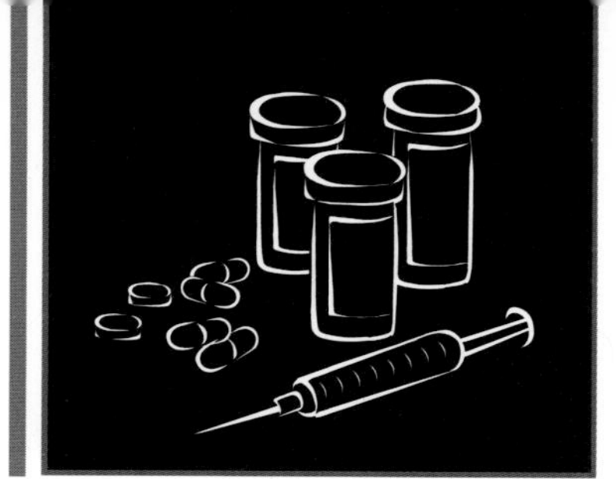

Drug Abuse and Teens

A Hot Issue

Shelagh Ryan Masline

Enslow Publishers, Inc.

40 Industrial Road
Box 398
Berkeley Heights, NJ 07922
USA

PO Box 38
Aldershot
Hants GU12 6BP
UK

http://www.enslow.com

To my lovely daughter, Caitlin.

Library of Congress Cataloging-in-Publication Data

Masline, Shelagh A. R.
Drug abuse and teens : a hot issue / Shelagh Ryan Masline.
p. cm. — (Hot issues)
Includes bibliographical references and index.
Summary: Describes the harmful effects of the many illegal substances being used in the United States and offers ways to steer clear of drugs and to seek help if needed.
ISBN 0-7660-1372-3
1. Teenagers—Drug use—Juvenile literature. 2. Teenagers—Substance use—Juvenile literature. 3. Drug abuse—Prevention—Juvenile literature. 4. Substance abuse—Prevention—Juvenile literature. [1. Drug abuse.] I. Title. II. Series.

HV5824.Y68 M373 2000
362.29'0835 21—dc21

99-041408

Printed in the United States of America

10 9 8 7 6 5 4 3 2 1

To Our Readers:
All Internet addresses in this book were active and appropriate when we went to press. Any comments or suggestions can be sent by e-mail to Comments@enslow.com or to the address on the back cover.

Illustration Credits: AP/Wide World Photos, pp. 9, 19, 24, 41, 42; Corbis Digital Stock, p. 46; Skjold Photographs, pp. 15, 29, 32, 51.

Cover Illustration: Corbis Digital Stock

Contents

Chapter 1

What Is Drug Abuse?

In the late afternoon of January 29, 1999, a horrific car crash took the lives of five teenage girls. The accident happened in a middle-class suburb southwest of Philadelphia. Grief-stricken friends and classmates from nearby Penncrest High School, where the girls were juniors, later gathered at the scene of the accident. They left messages like "We love you all," "Forever rest in peace," and "I will always love you" at the bottom of the tree. The girls' Chevrolet Corsica had hit the tree with such force that the bark had been stripped clean by the impact.

The girls—Loren Wells, Tracy Graham, Rachel Lehr, Shaena Grigaitis, and Rebecca Weirich—were bright and popular. No one had expected them to die so young and so tragically. But friends, families, and school officials were in for another shock. A week after the accident, autopsies showed that the driver, sixteen-year old Loren, and at least three of the other girls, appeared to have been under the influence of a poisonous inhalant. Sniffing or inhaling chemicals (or inhalants) is a common and dangerous form of drug abuse by young people.

Neither the principal of Penncrest High nor the girls' teachers suspected that the girls were using inhalants. Even the parents of the dead teens sought to find a different explanation. They did not want to believe that drug abuse was involved. But an empty can of a spray used to clean computer keyboards was found in the car. Autopsies of the bodies revealed traces of a chemical found in that spray. The medical examiner said that "driver impairment, with the loss of control on a straight road in daylight, in good weather, with no other traffic involved, resulted not from youthful inexperience and a dangerous stretch of road, but primarily from intoxication due to inhalant abuse."[1]

Sadly, families, teachers, and friends do not always recognize that a young person has a problem with drugs until it is too late. But the fact is that substance abuse among teens rose sharply in the 1990s.[2] Today, two out of every ten eighth graders admits to having tried an inhalant.[3] By the time they reach their senior year in high school, more than a third of American teens has used marijuana, according to the National Institute on Drug Abuse.[4]

Young people in America are beginning to smoke cigarettes, drink alcohol, and use marijuana and other illegal drugs at younger ages than ever before.[5] Drugs are also more easily available today than they were in the past. President Clinton called the dramatic jump in drug use by young people in the 1990s "the ultimate threat to the future of our country."[6]

Drug abuse is the improper use of any drug for nonmedical purposes. The most recent wave of

Flowers, teddy bears, and letters were left at the foot of a tree where five Penncrest High School girls died in a car crash involving inhalant abuse. Notice how the tree's bark was stripped off by the force of the impact.

recreational drug use began in the 1960s. During that decade, young people rebelled against their parents and teachers by listening to rock and roll, protesting the Vietnam War, and smoking marijuana. Drugs were popular and even fashionable among many teens at that time. Perhaps, it was because the damaging and sometimes deadly effects of drugs were less well known and publicized than they are today. Although many people still associate drug abuse with the 1960s and 1970s, it would be a mistake to think that the problem ever really went away.

Drug Abuse Today

After a promising decline throughout the 1980s and early 1990s, drug use once again began to rise.[7] Alcohol and cigarettes are the drugs most frequently abused by teens today. However, marijuana is becoming more popular.[8] More and more younger children are also trying inhalants.[9] Even drugs that are legal—for example, over-the-counter cough syrups—can be abused if they are taken to get high rather than to soothe a cough.

The Stages of Abuse

Drug abuse by teenagers tends to follow a pattern. Beer and wine are usually the first drugs that teens experiment with, followed by tobacco and hard liquor.[10] Next, marijuana may be tried, often in combination with alcohol.[11] Other illegal drugs—such as LSD and heroin—may be used after or along with marijuana.

Alcohol, tobacco (which contains the addictive substance nicotine), and marijuana are all gateway drugs. They can lead to the abuse of more dangerous substances. Of course, this does not mean that all teens follow the same pattern. Drinking beer or smoking marijuana does not always lead to abusing more serious substances.

Usually, drug abuse by teens falls into the following categories: experimental use, social recreational use, circumstantial use, intensified use, and compulsive use.[12]

Experimental use. Some teens try drugs just once or twice. But experimenting with drugs is a

Trends in Teen Drug Abuse

- ✓ Annual use of illegal drugs by high school seniors declined to a low of 27 percent in 1992, and then climbed steadily to 42 percent in 1997. It has remained steady since then.
- ✓ Annual marijuana use by high school seniors dropped to 27.1 percent in 1992, but rose steadily to 38.5 percent in 1997. It has remained steady since then.
- ✓ Annual cocaine use among high school seniors peaked at 13 percent in 1985, and then declined to just under 5 percent in 1996. It has remained steady since then.
- ✓ Probably due to the recent availability of cheap, high-quality heroin that can be snorted rather than injected, annual heroin use among high school seniors rose from 0.4 percent in 1991 to 1 percent in 1998.

Source: National Institute on Drug Abuse (NIDA), Monitoring the Future Study conducted by the University of Michigan Institute for Social Research, 1998, <http://www.nida.nih.gov> (September 1999).

risky business. Tragically, many young people do not survive their first experience with "huffing" or sniffing inhalants such as spray paint or gasoline. Most regular drug users started by "just experimenting" and then became hooked.

Social recreational use. Other teens get high only when they get together with their friends or go to parties. Unfortunately, recreational use of drugs can be harmful to young, developing bodies. It may also lead to greater abuse.

Circumstantial use. In some cases, teens use drugs in specific situations, such as to overcome shyness on a first date or to pull an all-nighter before a test. However, even short-term use of drugs is dangerous, and it can lead to more serious abuse.

Intensified use. This is the regular, habitual use of drugs for a long time. Signs of this very serious type of abuse include weight loss, fatigue, irritability, and frequent colds and sore throats.

Compulsive use. Compulsive users are prisoners of their habits. They may experience blackouts, or periods of time that a person cannot remember. Relationships with friends and family can grow tense and uncomfortable. Run-ins with the law may result from aggressive behavior, buying drugs, or stealing in order to buy drugs.

The Personal Consequences of Drug Abuse

Drugs can quickly have a negative impact on every aspect of a young person's life. The consequences are often both physical and psychological.

The physical consequences. The physical consequences of drug abuse can range from fatigue and irritability to overdose and death. Different

Police Crack Down on Marijuana Smokers

Because marijuana is a gateway drug to the abuse of more addictive and dangerous drugs, law enforcement agencies around the country are cracking down on people caught with even a small amount of this drug. A few years ago, a person caught smoking marijuana might simply have been told to throw away the joint. But if you are caught smoking marijuana in New York City today, where the possession of marijuana is a misdemeanor (a minor crime or offense), you will be held in custody from sixteen to thirty-six hours. You may be fingerprinted and strip-searched, and the police will check for any outstanding warrants against you.

Source: Kevin Flynn, "Arrests Soar in Crackdown on Marijuana," *The New York Times*," November 17, 1998, p. B1.

drugs cause different physical effects. Marijuana impairs judgment and motor skills and can cause lung damage. Regular use of stimulants, such as cocaine, can lead to insomnia, paranoia, appetite loss, and depression. Injecting any drug with shared, contaminated needles can cause life-threatening diseases. These diseases include AIDS (acquired immunodeficiency syndrome, a fatal disease that is spread through body fluids) and hepatitis (a serious liver disease).[13]

The worst physical consequence is death. Cocaine and crack claim victims from overdose, heart attack, or stroke. Hallucinogens cause strange and sometimes violent behavior. People have injured and killed themselves or others while under the influence of hallucinogens. Heroin and other narcotics can slow a user's breathing and heart rate so much that they simply stop. A street dealer may sell something that appears to be heroin but is actually a synthetic copy ten times more powerful. The risk of overdose from a designer drug like this is very high. Indirectly, abuse can lead to drug-related car accidents, drownings, falls, burns, and suicides.

The psychological consequences. Relationships with friends and family are often damaged when drugs enter a teen's life. Arguments can be frequent and intense. It is very common for teens to resent and turn away from people who are trying to help. Schoolwork suffers too, as loss of interest and lack of motivation cause grades to slip. As concentration and memory deteriorate, teens may skip school, fail courses, and eventually drop out altogether.

Substance abuse breaks down inhibitions, leading some young people to participate in unwanted and/or unprotected sex.[14] This can lead not only to life-threatening illnesses but also to unwanted pregnancies. Pregnant girls addicted to crack or heroin give birth to low-birth-weight infants suffering from painful addictions.

Teens who do drugs tend to hang out with other teens who do drugs. They abandon former friends. Some teenagers, male and female, eventually turn to prostitution to support their drug habits. Others steal, first from family, then from friends and strangers. The craving for drugs drives some young people to a range of desperate acts they would never have dreamed of doing before they got involved with drugs.

Many addicts will turn to crime to get money to buy drugs.

The Cost to Society

Drugs pose a serious threat not only to individuals but also to society. When drug use is common, there is usually an increase in violent crime. Innocent bystanders are wounded or killed in drug-related drive-by shootings. Children are killed by drunk drivers. Store owners are robbed by addicts who need money to buy drugs. In fact, half of all violent crimes are linked to substance abuse. Often the perpetrator, the victim, or both were drinking or using drugs when the crime was committed. A third of the arrests in the United States are drug- or alcohol-related.[15]

Chapter 2

Abuse of Legal Substances

When people think about drugs, they often imagine illegal substances such as marijuana or crack or heroin. They may picture dirty, unshaven junkies shooting up in the dark alleys of big cities. But many middle-class suburban kids also abuse drugs like marijuana and heroin. Illegal substances, however, are not the only a problem. Teens also abuse a wide variety of legal substances.

When used improperly, medications such as cough syrup and laxatives are just as damaging—and sometimes even as deadly—as illegal drugs. Medications are not the only legal substances subject to abuse. Teens in search of a quick, cheap, and accessible high are sometimes tempted to inhale or "huff" the fumes of common household products. Or they abuse dietary supplements like steroids and herbs to build muscle, lose weight, or feel more at ease at parties. Finally, they may turn to alcohol or tobacco, legal substances for adults but not for teens. Abusing these substances is dangerous and risky. It can also lead to involvement with illegal drugs.

Prescription and Over-the-Counter Drug Abuse

More than $78 billion worth of legal drugs are produced in the United States every year.[1] Although most of these prescription and over-the-counter remedies are taken correctly, a significant number are taken for nonmedical reasons. In 1995, more than 21 million people over the age of twelve admitted using a prescription drug for a nonmedical purpose, according to a survey conducted by the Substance Abuse and Mental Health Services Administration (SAMHSA).[2]

Young people abuse legal drugs in many different ways. Some individuals sell their own prescription drugs on the street or at school. Others take more medication than they are supposed to or take it incorrectly.

Most common, legal drugs are abused when they are taken for the wrong reasons. For example, instead of taking a painkiller to ease a toothache, a person might take it just to feel relaxed and mellow. Laxatives are often abused by teenage girls who want to lose weight. Stimulants are taken by teens to stay awake all night to study or party. Cough syrup is consumed for its alcohol content, which may be as high as 40 percent.

Amphetamines and other stimulants. Amphetamines are stimulants taken to combat physical and mental fatigue. Many are prescribed as diet pills. In the 1980s, ballet dancer Gelsey Kirkland regularly took a combination of amphetamines and cocaine to keep her weight down and inspire her dancing. However, she was forced to retire and enter a mental hospital when her addiction made her suicidal.

Amphetamines such as Benzedrine ("bennies"),

Dexedrine ("dexies"), and biphetamine ("black Cadillacs") are powerful stimulants that make people feel as if they have more energy, endurance, and speed. Although some are legal and can be obtained by prescription, amphetamines have become more strictly regulated over the years because of their highly addictive quality. As a result, many amphetamines are now manufactured in illegal labs and sold on the street.

Other stimulants include ephedrine, caffeine, and phenylpropanolamine. Large doses of these stimulants, which are found in over-the-counter diet pills and certain cold and allergy medications, can cause restlessness, sleeplessness, and diarrhea. Taking them over long periods of time can lead to dependency. In fact, even someone who drinks caffeinated coffee or soda regularly may experience withdrawal symptoms such as irritability when those beverages are not available.[3]

At low doses, stimulants increase heart and breathing rates so a person feels more alert. High doses can lead to dizziness, sleeplessness, blurred vision, and an irregular heartbeat. Psychological effects include anxiety, moodiness, and restlessness. Over time, habitual use of stimulants can lead to hallucinations and paranoia. Overdose can cause stroke or heart failure.

Tranquilizers, sedatives, and other depressants. Tranquilizers and sedatives are depressants. They lower blood pressure and slow down the metabolism, brain, and nervous system. When used correctly, tranquilizers relieve anxiety, and sedatives help a person get a good night's sleep. But like all other drugs, they can be abused.

The popular tranquilizer Valium was thought to

be a safe, nonaddictive substance when it was first introduced in 1963. It quickly became one of the best-selling prescription drugs of all time. The use of tranquilizers became so common that the rock group The Rolling Stones wrote a song about them called "Mother's Little Helper."[4] In the 1980s, Valium gave way to Xanax. But Xanax, too, has become a widely abused drug in the United States because it is highly addictive.

Over time, even normal amounts of tranquilizers and sedatives can lead to feelings of extreme sluggishness, lethargy, and fatigue. Large doses can cause confusion, altered perceptions, slurred

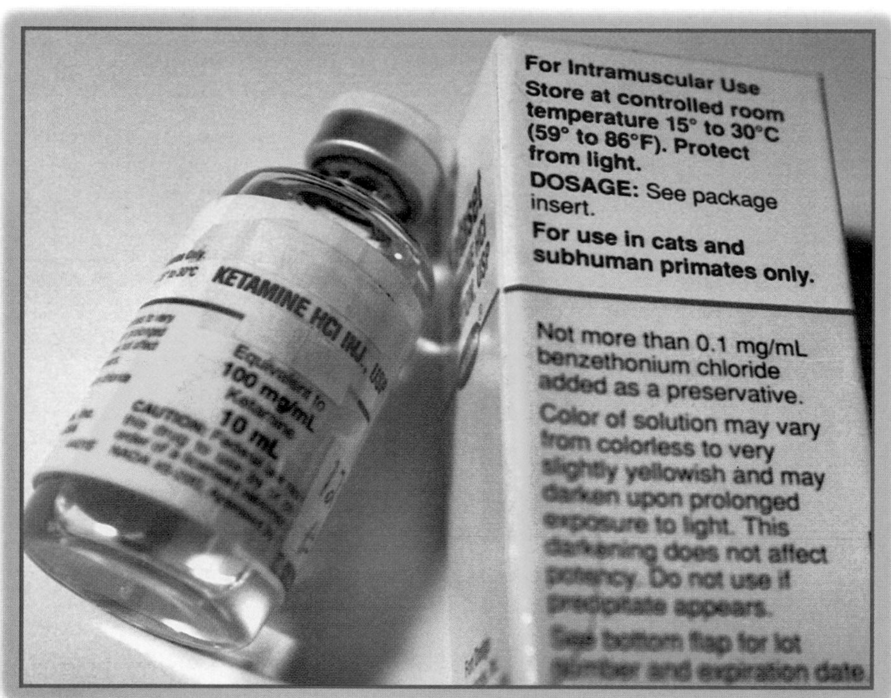

Some teenagers abuse the animal tranquilizer ketamine hydrochloride (called "Special K" by the drug culture) to get high. It is not meant for human use.

speech, loss of motor control, and depression. Overuse can lead to breathing difficulties, insomnia, coma, and even death. Tranquilizers and sedatives can be extremely addictive. Withdrawal from them causes severe anxiety and sleeplessness.

Other depressants include alcohol, narcotics, and barbiturates. Depressants are cross-addictive: If one type of depressant is not available, an addict will turn to another type. Former First Lady Betty Ford, who founded a clinic for addicts, abused depressants. Depressants—legal and illegal—have played a role in the deaths of many people, including the celebrities Elvis Presley, Judy Garland, Marilyn Monroe, John Belushi, and River Phoenix.

Narcotics. Narcotics, or opiates, are powerful painkilling and sedative drugs. Certain narcotics made from opium poppies, such as morphine and codeine, are legal. Synthetically manufactured Demerol, Dilaudid, and Percocet are also legal. Because of their intensely addictive nature, however, all these drugs are very strictly regulated. Other narcotics, such as heroin, are strictly illegal.

Legal narcotics can effectively control severe pain, such as that following surgery. But because they are so powerful and addictive, doctors are careful to administer only low doses of narcotics for short periods. High doses of narcotics can lead to extreme drowsiness, and users risk lapsing into a coma. Since a tolerance to narcotics develops over time, larger and larger doses are required to get high. But dosage is tricky, and overdose can result in death.

Antidepressants. Antidepressants are prescribed to treat some of the approximately 18 million individuals stricken with depression each year.[5]

Should Marijuana Be Legalized for Medical Use?

Smoking marijuana is said to reduce nausea in people who undergo chemotherapy for cancer. It may also control eye pressure in glaucoma patients and reduce spasms in paraplegics and people who have neurological diseases such as multiple sclerosis (MS). For these reasons, many people believe that marijuana should be made legal for medical use. In the November 1998 elections, people in Alaska, Arizona, Nevada, Oregon, and Washington followed Californians in voting to legalize marijuana for medical use in their states.

These votes are controversial and likely to face many court challenges before access to medical marijuana ever happens. Many people believe that the medical use of marijuana opens the door to even more serious drug abuse and crime. "There have been no reputable studies that propose to demonstrate marijuana's medicinal qualities," says Jim McDonough, director of Strategy for the White House Drug Control Office. He continues:

> *The seduction of medical marijuana makes it seem that marijuana is both harmless and beneficial. That sends a bad message and encourages abuse. In the 1970s, Alaska allowed home use of marijuana. There was a marked increase of use by young people and a rise in child crime. [Alaska repealed that law in 1990.]*

The executive director of the National Council for Drug Control, Sam Vagenas, does not believe that the medical use of marijuana leads to its abuse. He says:

> *Recent figures from the Department of Health and Human Services in California [where medical use of marijuana is legal] show that teenagers in California are actually less likely to abuse marijuana: 6.9 percent of California teenagers 12 to 17 used marijuana often, while 9.9 percent of teenagers nationally used it frequently.*

Source: "Marijuana Votes: Bane or Benefit?" *The New York Times*, November 17, 1998, p. F9.

Depression is a serious disease. Antidepressants are designed to control depression by changing the function and structure of brain tissue. Unlike physically addictive drugs such as tranquilizers and narcotics, antidepressants have had little potential for drug abuse. However, there is some controversy surrounding a new class of antidepressants that includes the popular Prozac. Some experts have been concerned that Prozac has mind-altering qualities. Fortunately, recent research shows that Prozac does not actually change someone's personality. It can just seem that way if a person has been depressed for a long time and is finally getting back to his or her normal self.

Inhalants

Some adolescents huff the fumes of inhalants to get a quick, cheap high. Inhalants include common household products, such as butane from cigarette lighters, gasoline, glue, paint thinner, aerosol sprays, and antifreeze. Nitrous oxide ("laughing gas"), amyl nitrate ("snappers" or "poppers"), and butyl nitrate ("bullet," or "rush") are also popular inhalants.

Inhalant abuse is increasing every year, and younger adolescents are particularly vulnerable to the problem. They seem to believe that, because inhalants are often ordinary household substances, they are not harmful. Unfortunately, nothing could be further from the truth. Huffing can have very serious consequences. Even first-time users run the risk of death.

The short-term effects of inhalants include slurred speech, lack of coordination, heart palpitations, trouble breathing, dizziness, and headache. Over time, using inhalants can lead to damage of the lungs, liver, and heart. Inhalants may cause memory loss, severe depression, psychosis, and other severe and permanent brain damage. Bizarre, reckless, and potentially deadly behavior can be the consequence of even one incident of abuse. Death can result from suffocation, choking on vomit, sudden sniffing death syndrome, or engaging in reckless behavior under the influence of inhalants.[6]

Dietary Supplements

In the United States, dietary supplements are largely unregulated. These supplements are not just dieting aids, but include various products such as anabolic steroids and herbal remedies in addition to the standard vitamins and minerals. Although in time this may change, dietary supplements do not have to be tested, approved, or inspected by the Food and Drug Administration (FDA) or any other federal agency.[7]

Steroids. Some athletes, at both the amateur and professional levels, take anabolic steroids—including the male hormone testosterone and its artificial derivatives—to increase muscle strength and gain weight. Some steroids are legal, over-the-counter supplements, while others are sold illegally on the street. But whether legal or illegal, there are serious problems with steroids. They can make a person feel angry, paranoid, and tense. Habitual use can lead to high blood pressure, sterility, an enlarged heart, liver disease, and death. Steroids can damage the bones of adolescents, resulting in stunted growth. Severe acne is another consequence. Males who take steroids may experience testicular shrinkage and develop breasts; females can grow facial hair, and their voices may deepen.

Some popular athletes have taken steroids. Mark McGwire helped revive the stale image of baseball in the summer of 1998. He and Sammy Sosa slugged it out to see who would beat Roger Maris's long-standing home-run record. But to some, McGwire's accomplishment of hitting seventy home runs was overshadowed by his use of a legal drug. McGwire was taking the testosterone-boosting, body-building steroid called androstenedione.[8] "Andro" is a legal over-the-counter supplement and is not banned by

For many fans, Mark McGwire's homerun record was overshadowed by his use of the legal body-building steroid called androstenedione. McGwire, however, has since stopped using the substance.

baseball. However, McGwire stopped taking it at the start of the following season because of all the negative publicity. "I got tired of hearing about young kids under age who were probably taking it improperly," he said.[9]

In recent years the Tour de France bicycle race has also been haunted by steroid use. In 1998, one team of cyclists from Iowa was expelled for using performance-enhancing drugs. A Dutch team, under suspicion, quit. In November of that year, the International Olympic Committee took a firm stand against performance-enhancing drugs. Committee members warned soccer, cycling, and tennis federations that their sports could be dropped from the Olympics if they did not obey antidrug rules.[10]

Herbs. Herbalism uses remedies prepared from the roots and leaves of plants. But just because they are natural does not mean that all plant remedies are harmless. Herbs have a significant impact on the body and must be treated with the same caution as any medication. In recent years, herbs such as ephedra (which is also known as ma huang) have been abused as quick weight-loss fixes. Yet responsible herbalists do not recommend ephedra for weight loss, and this herb has been banned by the United States Olympic Committee. The side effects of normal doses include restlessness, insomnia, headache, irritability, and nausea. Large amounts of ephedra can lead to fatal high blood pressure and heart rhythm disorders.

Alcohol and Tobacco

Because they are relatively cheap and easy to get, alcohol and cigarettes are typically the first drugs abused by young people. Thirty-four percent of fourth graders have experimented with alcohol, and 40 percent feel pressured to smoke cigarettes, according to the American Council for Drug Education.[11] But drinking alcohol is illegal for young people under twenty-one, and using tobacco is illegal under the age of eighteen. These drugs have dangerous health and social consequences and can lead to the abuse of even more serious and unsafe substances.

Alcohol. Alcoholism is a disease. "Long-term effects of heavy alcohol use include loss of appetite, vitamin deficiencies, stomach ailments, skin problems, sexual impotence, liver damage, heart and central nervous system damage and memory loss," warns the Federal Center for Substance Abuse Prevention.

In addition to health concerns, drinking can lead to a variety of other problems. "Nearly half of all deaths among those 15 to 19 years old involve traffic accidents in which alcohol was a factor," according to the American Academy of Pediatrics. Alcohol can also damage relationships with family and friends and impair school and job performance. It has been linked with acquaintance rape and unplanned pregnancy. A person who is arrested for driving while intoxicated (DWI) can have his or her license taken away, and repeat offenses can lead to jail time.

Binge drinking. Binge drinking—having five or more drinks in a row—is a potentially fatal practice among teens. People who drink like this are poisoning their bodies with alcohol. Yet almost half of the 9 million Americans under twenty-one who drank alcohol in 1996 were binge drinkers. In addition, 15.6 percent of eighth graders engaged in regular binge drinking in 1996, up from 12.9 percent in 1991.[12]

The truth about tobacco. Smoking is responsible for some four hundred fifty thousand deaths every year, and as many as one in five teenagers is a regular smoker, according to the Federal Center for Substance Abuse Prevention.[13] Risks associated with smoking include emphysema, heart disease, stroke, and cancer.

The number of young males who use smokeless tobacco is also on the rise.[14] Yet it is wrong to think that smokeless tobacco and snuff (finely ground tobacco) are harmless. Like cigarettes, smokeless tobacco is addictive. It can lead to cancer, cardiovascular difficulties, and other serious health problems.

Cigarettes and other forms of tobacco—including cigars, chew, snuff, and dip—all contain nicotine. There is evidence that addiction to nicotine leads to other forms of addiction. Experts at the Center for Substance Abuse Prevention now believe that teen smokers are "100 times more likely to smoke marijuana and are more likely to use other illicit drugs such as cocaine and heroin in the future."[15] More teens today are combining tobacco and drugs. Some smoke cigarettes after marijuana to enhance the high. Others hollow out cigars and replace the tobacco with marijuana.

Oftentimes, abusing legal drugs is not enough. Some teens move on to illegal drugs, which are often more dangerous.

Chapter 3

Illegal Drugs

In 1997, after nineteen of its young citizens died of heroin abuse in a single three-year period, Plano, Texas, became known as Heroin City, USA. Reflecting a national trend, middle-class kids, preppies, jocks, and cheerleaders were the first to become involved with heroin in this affluent Dallas suburb. Among the dead teens were an altar boy, a football player, and a girl who loved to read and travel. An undercover agent was finally placed in the high school, leading to the arrest of many drug dealers. Today, there is hope that the heroin problem in Plano is under control at last.[1]

Over the years, there have been significant changes in the patterns of illegal drug use among young people. The National Institute on Drug Abuse (NIDA) keeps track of these trends in its annual Monitoring the Future (MTF) Study. For example, heroin use has traditionally been low among teens. However, the sudden availability of cheaper, high-purity heroin that could be snorted rather than injected led to its use doubling among high school seniors between 1991 and 1998. Although the use of marijuana, cocaine, and heroin "bottomed out" in the early 1990s, the MTF found that use of these drugs has risen again at all grade levels. Fortunately, the figures for 1997 and 1998 suggest that the overall use of illegal drugs is once again leveling off.[2]

Marijuana and Hashish

Marijuana is made from the leaves and flowers of the Indian hemp plant. This drug was used as a natural healing aid in ancient India, China, and Africa. Hashish is a potent form of marijuana that is made from the sticky resin of the plant. It was smoked for centuries in Arabic countries to relieve headaches and intestinal pains. Even in the United States, nineteenth-century drugstores sold

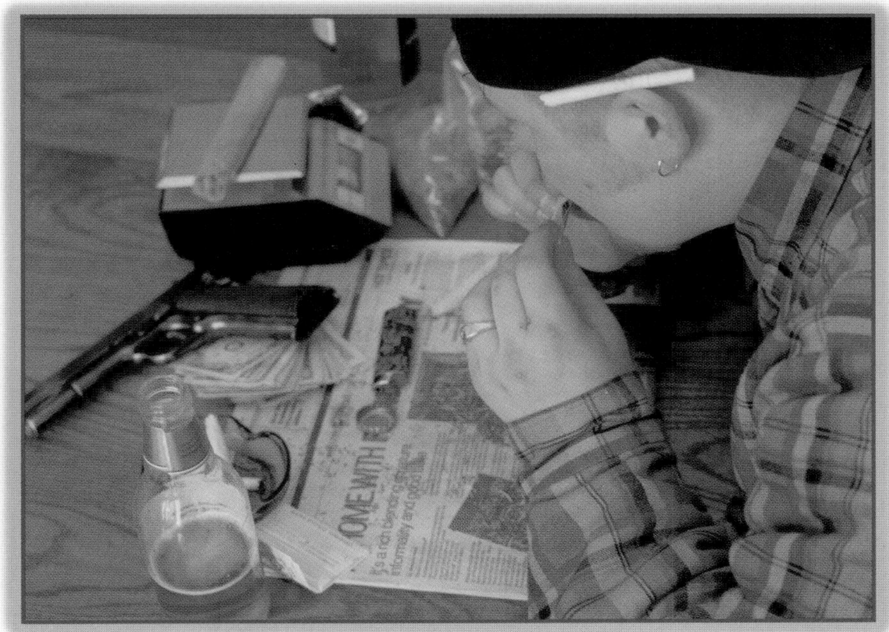

Many teens falsely believe that marijuana is harmless. The drug can damage short-term memory and cause breathing problems. Most habitual marijuana users do poorly in school.

commercial preparations of marijuana to treat coughs, insomnia, and migraine headaches. But as time went on and values changed, the drug was declared illegal in state after state during the 1930s.

Young people smoke marijuana to get high. They want to forget their troubles and feel happy. But marijuana is not harmless. Like smoking cigarettes, smoking marijuana causes lung cancer. Marijuana can damage short-term memory, impair judgment and motor skills, distort perceptions, lead to anxiety, and cause breathing problems. Habitual users do poorly in school and are more likely to drop out.

Marijuana use by high school seniors almost doubled in the 1990s, from 21.9 percent in 1992 to 38.5 percent in 1997.[3] The average age for the first use of marijuana is thirteen and a half.[4]

Heroin

Like marijuana, heroin had a respectable start. It was first sold in late nineteenth-century Germany by the Bayer Company. This is the same company that created safe and wholesome products like Bayer Aspirin for Children. Ironically, heroin's name comes from its supposedly "heroic" healing qualities. However, its extremely addictive nature makes heroin one of the most dangerous drugs of all. The craving for it is often so intense that teenage addicts rob, steal, and prostitute themselves to get money to buy heroin.

Although not nearly as popular as marijuana, heroin has experienced an alarming increase in use in recent years. The drug has become popular among middle-class teens in the suburbs, and celebrity use has also been in the news. Because the drug is purer than in the past, it is now possible to smoke and snort heroin as well as inject it. In the past, users probably steered clear of heroin due to a fear of AIDS. This life-threatening virus is transmitted via shared, contaminated needles. Yet the truth is that there is no safe way to use heroin.

Heroin—also called dope, Big H, horse, boy, and smack—turns into morphine in a user's body. It works by simultaneously activating pleasure centers in the brain and depressing the central nervous system. The initial high or "rush" of this drug brings on a sudden feeling of euphoria (a feeling of extreme well-being, vigor, and health). Afterward, users appear sleepy and peaceful, as if they are "nodding out." Depending on several factors, nodding out can lead to serious heart and breathing problems and even coma or death. These factors include the amount and purity of the heroin taken, whether heroin is taken along with alcohol or other drugs, and the susceptibility of the user.

Heroin creates a deadly cycle of abuse. As soon as the pleasurable feelings it brings on fade, the user craves more of the drug. Habitual use leads to a loss of interest in former friends and hobbies, food, and basically anything else besides getting high. Addicts quickly build up a tolerance. This means that they need larger and larger amounts of the drug to get high. Overdose is a constant risk. Withdrawal is long, painful, and often unsuccessful. It involves stomach cramps, vomiting, diarrhea, muscle spasms, sweats, and an uncontrollable sensation of insects crawling all over the body.

Cocaine

Whereas heroin makes people nod out, cocaine—a stimulant—causes the opposite effect. It increases

After an initial feeling of intense happiness, heroin users feel sleepy. As soon as these feelings stop, the user has an overwhelming need to take more of the drug.

blood pressure, heart rate, breathing rate, and body temperature. Cocaine is a white powder made from the leaves of the South American coca plant. It is also known as coke, blow, toot, and nose candy. As the heart races and blood pressure climbs, cocaine can lead to seizures or heart attacks in susceptible individuals. Unfortunately, there is no way to know who is susceptible or not until it is too late.

Like heroin, cocaine is highly addictive. At first, it provides brief but intense sensations of well-being, self-confidence, and exhilaration. But these pleasurable feelings only last fifteen to thirty minutes. They are followed by a "crash" or period of depression.

This crash is intense and lasts much longer than the high before it. As they are "coming down," users feel uncomfortable, edgy, and paranoid. They crave more cocaine to avoid crashing.[5]

Cravings to get high again can become so intense that they begin to dominate every aspect of an addict's life. Habitual use can lead to chronic insomnia, paranoia, appetite loss, and depression.

Freebasing. Some people choose to inject cocaine or smoke it in a water pipe. Although there is no safe way to use cocaine, smoking it—which is called freebasing—is a very hazardous practice. Ether, which is used in the process, is highly flammable. When actor and comedian Richard Pryor lit a match to freebase cocaine, the ether caught fire, and he was covered with flames. Severely burned, Pryor almost died.[6]

Crack cocaine. Crack is a cheap, smokable form of cocaine. It is highly potent and addictive. Crack addiction affects both the body and the mind. It soon dominates every part of the addict's life because all he or she can think about is getting high.

When it first appeared in the 1980s, crack caused widespread social problems. Newspapers ran stories about "crack houses," or run-down, empty buildings where addicts met to buy crack and smoke it, often staying there for days. "Crack babies" were born addicted to the drug because their mothers used it when they were pregnant. Fortunately, today the crack epidemic seems to have run its course. It is not widely used by young people.[7]

Speedballs. Combining one drug with another is a very dangerous practice. Crack is sometimes mixed with heroin in powerful mixtures called speedballs, moon rocks, or parachutes. These combinations can be deadly, as shown by the sad and early deaths of talented actors River Phoenix and John Belushi.[8] But dangerous mixtures of drugs like these are nonetheless popular once more, especially among suburban teenagers.

Death at an early age. By the age of twenty-three, actor River Phoenix had already been featured in movies such as *Stand By Me*, *My Own Private Idaho*, and *Running on Empty*. On October 31, 1993, the young actor collapsed to the sidewalk, suffered a series of convulsions, and died outside the Viper Room, a Los Angeles nightclub. His younger brother, nineteen-year-old Joaquin, made a desperate call to 911, but it was too late to save River.

Robin Williams, star of movies such as *Mrs. Doubtfire* and *Good Will Hunting*, shook his head sadly when a reporter asked him about River's death. He explained that his own wild years had abruptly ended in 1982, after his friend John Belushi died of an overdose of cocaine and heroin. Williams had been with Belushi earlier that night at a Sunset Strip hotel.[9]

In an autopsy of River Phoenix, the coroner found lethal levels of cocaine and morphine (which is what heroin breaks down into) in Phoenix's body. The coroner also found traces of marijuana, Valium, and an over-the-counter cold medication. A spokeswoman for the late actor said, "Hopefully it's a wake-up call to the world. It leaves you to question why young people are compelled to do this. If any good can come from this death, it can come from saving someone's life."[10]

The Warning Signs of Drug Abuse

- ✓ Personality change
- ✓ Sudden mood changes
- ✓ Irresponsible behavior
- ✓ Low self-esteem
- ✓ Withdrawal
- ✓ Depression
- ✓ Fatigue
- ✓ Memory lapses
- ✓ Carelessness with grooming
- ✓ Irritability
- ✓ Hostility
- ✓ Starting arguments
- ✓ Deteriorating relationships with family and friends
- ✓ New friends who are less interested in former home and school activities
- ✓ A drop in grades at school
- ✓ Missing school
- ✓ Trouble with the law
- ✓ Loss of interest in favorite activities
- ✓ Changes in eating or sleeping patterns
- ✓ Changes in body weight, especially weight loss
- ✓ A persistent cough
- ✓ Sallow (grayish, greenish, or yellowish) skin
- ✓ Red and dull eyes
- ✓ Frequent use of eyedrops
- ✓ Use of incense and other deodorizers
- ✓ Signs of drugs and drug paraphernalia, such as rolling papers or plastic bags
- ✓ Clothing, posters, jewelry, or other items promoting drug use

Source: Adapted and expanded from National Institute on Drug Abuse, *Marijuana: Facts Parents Need to Know* (U.S. Department of Health and Human Services: NCADI Publication No. PHD712, 1995), pp. 8–10.

LSD and Other Hallucinogens

Hallucinogens are psychoactive or mind-altering drugs that distort a person's perception of reality. Lysergic acid diethylamide (LSD), also known as acid, first achieved popularity in the 1960s. Its use is fast growing among those under twenty years of age, according to the Drug Enforcement Administration (DEA). Teens say that they take LSD for a variety of reasons—because they are bored, to get high, to experiment, out of curiosity, or due to peer pressure.

Hallucinogens can produce bizarre, unpredictable, and sometimes violent behavior. Emotions swing dramatically under their influence. There may be hallucinations (imaginary sights) and delusions (fixed ideas that are incorrect but seem very real to the person experiencing them). People have injured and killed themselves and others after taking LSD and other hallucinogens. Even after the initial experience is over, some users suffer through the same hallucinations, trailing (seeing a trail of moving objects), and paranoia again in what are called flashbacks.

Although LSD is probably the most well-known hallucinogen, it is far from the only one. Other hallucinogens are natural substances, such as mescaline from the peyote plant and psilocybin from so-called magic mushrooms.

Some users find the images and feeling produced by hallucinogens to be inspiring and exciting. However, many others find these experiences terrifying. "I know of kids who had bad trips," said Duane B. (not his real name). "One said that when he took LSD, he felt that he had turned into a potato chip and would crumble into pieces because he was so fragile."[11]

Hallucinogens alter the user's perception of time, space, distance, and mood. "I found that I couldn't make many decisions on acid, or I'd feel overwhelmed," explained Duane,

> Taking acid made it seem that going through the motions of daily life was a huge labor. Just getting dressed took forever. Going through these simple actions was so complicated that I wondered if it was worth the effort of putting on my socks and shoes.[12]

Young people can develop a psychological addiction to hallucinogens. This means that even though these drugs are not physically addictive, one can get into a habit of using these drugs that is hard to break. It was only with help that Duane was able to stop taking LSD.

Designer Drugs

Designer drugs are synthetic copies of amphetamines, narcotics, and hallucinogens. They are becoming increasingly popular among young people today. As with other illegal substances, teens take designer drugs for various reasons—to become relaxed and mellow, to experience an extra burst of energy, or to have a psychedelic, hallucinogenic experience. But over time, the use of these dangerous substances can lead to serious psychological problems such as anxiety, depression, and paranoia. Permanent brain damage, paralysis, addiction, convulsions, and death are all potential consequences.

Where did designer drugs come from? In the 1970s and early 1980s, designer drugs were manufactured to take advantage of a loophole in drug regulations. Drugs such as heroin were prohibited by the Controlled Substances Act of 1970, but synthetic copies of them were not. Designer drugs became a popular alternative to their strictly illegal counterparts. As their dangerous effects became increasingly evident, the law was tightened in 1985 to forbid the manufacture or use of any designer drugs.

Designer drugs pose dangerous risks for teens. No one knows exactly what will happen when a person takes a designer drug. Because they are manufactured by underground chemists in back rooms and garages, the effects of designer drugs on a person's mind and body are unpredictable. Contamination is common. Also, an unskilled "chemist" may produce a drug with very different effects from those intended. In the mid-1980s, an error in the makeup of a designer drug in California caused young people who used it to develop Parkinson's disease. This disease usually afflicts older people. Caused by the death of brain cells, it gradually paralyzes victims until they are no longer able to walk or talk or feed themselves.

Designer drugs often have exotic names, such as Angel Dust and Ecstasy. These names are deliberate marketing ploys to create images of mystery and romance, seducing teens into risky and illegal behavior. But the more a person knows about designer drugs, the better equipped he or she is to say no to them.

Angel dust (PCP). Seventeen-year-old Theresa grew up on the streets of the Bronx. Sent from home to home, she earned pocket money baby-sitting for the children of crack addicts. Sadly, Theresa turned to drugs such as PCP to help her forget her situation.[13]

Phencyclidine or PCP was developed in 1957 as an anesthetic to reduce surgical pain. The use of PCP was soon halted due to side effects such as delirium and confusion. Yet today, Los Angeles gangs manufacture a liquid form of PCP and ship it all around the country. Cigarettes of marijuana, parsley, oregano, or tobacco are dipped into PCP and sold on the street as Angel Dust, Killer Joints, Lethal Weapon, Purple Rain, and Rocket Fuel.

Theresa is more fortunate than many other addicts. She entered a treatment program and has been drug-free for a year. But the effects of PCP can vary greatly, and most PCP experiences end in disaster. In Upstate New York, a seventeen-year-old boy was stabbed to death by friends who accused him of stealing their PCP. In jail for the crime, one of his accused murderers hanged himself with a sheet.[14]

Under the influence of PCP, people have jumped out of buildings and driven their cars into oncoming traffic. They have committed violent acts that they had no memory of later. Like LSD, this dangerous designer hallucinogen distorts perceptions of reality and can cause psychotic reactions.

China White (Fentanyl). Fentanyl, a powerful legal narcotic, was developed to be used only in a controlled hospital setting. Doctors were not even allowed to write prescriptions for this drug, which is a thousand times more powerful than morphine. Yet today, designer copies of fentanyl such as China White are sold on the street.

China White looks like heroin and has the same effects on the body as heroin. People who snort, smoke, or inject this drug experience a surge of euphoria. It is followed by a peaceful period of nodding out. Yet China White is much more powerful than heroin. Consequently, people who believe they are using heroin may use too much. Overdose in some cases is so quick that addicts are found dead with the needles still hanging out of their veins.

Ecstasy (MDMA). Ecstasy is one of the most popular designer drugs among young people. It works by creating feelings of euphoria and heightened sensual awareness. Sold as a pill or a powder, Ecstasy's other street names include XTC, Adam, Clarity, E, and Essence.

MDMA—or 3-4-methylenedioxymethamphetamine—is the chemical name for Ecstasy. This drug was first developed by a German pharmaceutical company in 1914. However, World War I broke out soon afterward, and it never reached the marketplace. Originally intended as a diet aid, MDMA was probably retired because it caused too many negative side effects.

The Ecstasy experience often plays an important part in popular all-night dance parties called raves, where techno, jungle, and trance music are played. At raves held in abandoned warehouses and basements, the music throbs, lasers flash, and drug use is rampant. There Ecstasy is sometimes used with LSD in a combination called X&L or candy flips.

An average dose of Ecstasy creates an initial period of chills, sweating, and nausea. This is followed by several hours of extreme happiness, warmth, and tenderness. This has led to Ecstasy's nickname as the "hug drug." But some users have disturbing hallucinations, and the high is followed by a crash. This may consist of a day or as much as a week or two of anxiety, confusion, and depression.

The drug Ecstasy is used at all-night dance parties called raves. At raves, drug use is common among the party-goers (though the people in this photo are not necessarily under the influence of drugs).

Since Ecstasy, or MDMA, is made in people's basements, garages, and kitchens, each batch can have chemical differences. Sometimes Ecstasy is pure; other times it is mixed or cut with harmful contaminants. People can die from a bad dose of Ecstasy. Scientists at Johns Hopkins warn that heavy users can suffer long-lasting nerve cell damage in their brains.[15]

Speed (methamphetamine). In Arizona, sixteen-year-old high school student Heather started using methamphetamine after she was given a "free sample." This is a dealer's trick to get a young person hooked on drugs so that the dealer can then sell

This illegal methamphetamine lab was found by DEA agents in Oklahoma. Criminals use household items like batteries, Styrofoam cups, and over-the-counter cold medications to "cook" a batch of meth.

them to him or her. As Heather took more speed, her relationships with family and friends deteriorated. She lost her sense of self-worth. Eventually she dropped out of school and was placed in a treatment program.[16]

Illegal underground labs in California are currently flooding the West Coast with this strong stimulant. This drug, more powerful than amphetamine, is easy to manufacture. There are many names for methamphetamine, depending on the ingredients used and the "recipe" followed to make it. The most common names are meth, crystal meth, speed, crank, and ice. Meth is usually in powder or crystal form. It can be smoked, inhaled, eaten, or injected intravenously.

Meth is appealing to teens because it creates feelings of intense happiness and euphoric well-being. These effects can last for up to sixteen hours. Use of methamphetamine in California is highest among white teenage males who are nicknamed "speed freaks."[17] Since it is cheaper and longer lasting, many young people are opting for meth instead of cocaine. In fact, methamphetamine is often called the poor man's cocaine.

Methamphetamine is highly addictive and tolerance develops quickly. As with cocaine, the user is driven to do more and more of the drug to avoid crashing. Even when high, the side effects of meth-induced euphoria can include panic, paranoia, and hallucinations. Years after a serious addict quits, he or she may continue to experience flashbacks. Addicts can also become violent.

Chapter 4

Why Do Teens Do Drugs?

Teens abuse alcohol and drugs for many different reasons. Some are curious about what it feels like to "get high." Others think drugs will relax them, increase their self-confidence, or make them more popular with their friends. Many teens take drugs because they are trying to fit in with a particular group in their neighborhood or at school. In other cases, young people drink beer or smoke cigarettes to assert their independence and rebel against their parents.[1] Understanding the signs of drug abuse and the reasons for it can help teens steer clear of this serious problem.

Family Problems

Teens who grow up in troubled families are at a greater risk of becoming involved with drugs. When alcohol, tobacco, or drugs are used in a home, a young person is also more likely to abuse these substances. Teens resent double standards, and easy access to illicit substances is often too tempting to resist.

Other family issues can also contribute to drug abuse. Teens whose parents divorce, for example, may attempt to escape emotional pain and pressure by using drugs. Absent parents or parents who fight a lot are another risk factor. A lack of clearly set and agreed-on rules, inconsistent discipline, and parents who are either too strict or too lenient can also put a teen at risk for drug use. Teens who have suffered sexual abuse (which usually involves a close relative or family friend) are also more likely to get involved with drugs.[2]

Peer Pressure

As young people enter adolescence, the importance and influence of friends skyrockets. Adolescents need to feel part of a group. This need makes them susceptible to peer pressure. Teens may try to

Why Teens Use Drugs

- ✓To be more popular with friends
- ✓So people will like them
- ✓Because their parents use(d) them
- ✓Because someone else wanted them to
- ✓To make them feel more like adults
- ✓Because their friends use(d) drugs

Source: J. Novacek, R. Raskin, and R. Hogan, "Why Do Adolescents Use Drugs? Age, Sex, and User Differences," *Journal of Youth and Adolescence*, vol. 20, p. 476.

Family problems or a lack of supportive friends can put a teen at risk for drug or alcohol abuse.

influence their friends to cut school, cheat on a test, or engage in some other sort of wrong or risky behavior. The pressure to drink alcohol, smoke cigarettes, or use drugs is one of the most dangerous types of peer pressure.

How much pressure a teen feels to experiment with drugs depends on the nature of his or her friends. If time is spent with others who share positive interests, there will be less pressure. If friends use drugs, a teen is under greater pressure to experiment with them.[3]

Low Self-esteem and Other Issues

Young people with a strong sense of self are best able to resist peer pressure and say no to drugs. Teens who suffer from low self-esteem, feel they do not fit in with their peers, or start having sex at an early age are more likely to abuse alcohol and drugs.[4] Teens who are naturally defiant, aggressive, or impulsive are also at risk.

The Challenges of Adolescence

Some teens are tempted to rely on drugs as a way of facing the challenges of adolescence. Adolescence is a period of great physical and emotional growth. Coping with the changes that adolescence brings can be stressful and confusing to young people. Yet using drugs is not a good way to feel more self-confident, win friends, or feel more relaxed at parties. Teens who do this do not learn the valuable emotional, psychological, and social lessons of adolescence. They reach adulthood without having developed the same coping skills and strategies as drug-free teens.[5] Young people in this situation also place themselves at a more immediate risk of drug-related accidents and even death.

However, it is never too late to get help. Along with the family, trusted adults can help a teen come to terms with a drug problem. There are also many organizations that can help a person resist drugs, stop recreational use of them, or kick an addiction.

Chapter 5

How to Get Help

Young people today are being exposed to drugs at an earlier age—even in elementary school. To make matters worse, it is getting easier for underage kids to obtain alcohol, tobacco, and illegal drugs.

Fortunately, there are many steps a teen can take to avoid becoming involved with drugs. And, even if a teen is already smoking cigarettes, drinking beer, sniffing inhalants, or even shooting heroin, help is available to beat addiction.

The Importance of Family

Honesty, trust, and communication within the family are strong protections against drug abuse. Busy as we all are today, more families are making a point to sit down to dinner together and share what is happening in one another's lives.

Choose a Mentor

The love and support of one caring adult can help teens successfully navigate their way through adolescence. If not a parent, this person can be an aunt or uncle, grandparent, teacher, school psychologist, guidance counselor, minister, rabbi, physician, or other mentor. A mentor is a person who listens to a teen's private thoughts and concerns without criticizing the teen. He or she helps the teen develop positive ways of dealing with problems. Teens can freely express their thoughts and feelings to the right mentor.

Resist Peer Pressure

Young people are sometimes pressured into using alcohol or other drugs by their friends. Fortunately, there are many ways to resist peer pressure. It is important for teens to realize that they have certain rights.

All teens have the power to decide what they think is right or wrong for themselves and express their own opinions. Teens have the right to say no and mean it. They are responsible for their own feelings and have the right to change their minds and walk away from an undesirable situation if they want.[1]

Get Involved in Extracurricular Activities

When peers use drugs, there is more pressure to "at least try them." Instead, it is a good idea to spend time with friends who share positive interests such as sports, movies, music, art, dance, chess, or other hobbies. There will be less pressure this way. In addition, teens who participate in clubs, teams, and other extracurricular activities develop a greater resistance to drugs, because these hobbies are a healthy outlet for stress and help build self-esteem.[2]

The caring and support of a mentor can help a teen resist the pressure to use drugs.

Develop Self-esteem

Self-esteem means feeling good about oneself. Young people who feel comfortable with who they are and are proud of their achievements are better able to resist negative peer pressure. They are also less influenced by manipulative advertising that portrays tobacco and alcohol use as sexy and appealing.

Self-esteem can come from many different sources. For example, some teens value education and a future career. They feel good about themselves because they do well in school. Others enjoy non-drug-associated extracurricular activities such as sports or dance. Active participation in sports, school clubs, arts and crafts classes, and volunteer activities can all keep teens busy and active and help prevent them from using drugs.[3] In addition, these are activities at which teens can meet friends who share their interests and values.

Learn More About Drugs

Knowing the consequences of drinking alcohol, smoking cigarettes, or using drugs can help teens make the correct decision to avoid these behaviors. Because young people tend to think they will live forever and often do not take the health risks of drugs seriously, there are many programs that teach the facts about drug abuse.

DARE and Other Antidrug Programs

Antidrug programs teach that drug abuse is dangerous and unacceptable. DARE (Drug Abuse Resistance Education) is probably the most well

How to Resist Peer Pressure

Young people are sometimes pressured into using alcohol or other drugs by their peers. But all teens have a right to

✓Decide what they think is right themselves and express their own opinions.

✓Be responsible for their own feelings.

✓Say no and mean no.

✓Leave a threatening or otherwise undesirable situation.

✓Change their minds and decide not to use drugs.

Source: Edward S. Traisman, ed., *American Medical Association Complete Guide to Your Children's Health* (New York: Random House, 1999), p. 196.

known antidrug program today. It sends uniformed police officers to schools to give lessons about drug abuse and resisting peer pressure. Popular DARE supplies include everything from bumper stickers to T-shirts.

Many schools and community groups are also exploring a variety of other antidrug programs. This is because some of the reports on DARE show mixed results, and the program has been criticized in recent years. DARE "does not make much of a dent in drug use when the kid gets older," points out Seattle police chief Norm Stamper.[4]

Support Groups and Rehabilitation Programs

For teens already involved with drugs, there are many helpful programs such as support groups and out-patient or live-in rehabilitation centers. Some are twelve-step programs, based on the Alcoholics Anonymous (AA) model, which help drug-addicted teens with their recovery. Research has found that recovery programs are most effective when they take place in age-appropriate peer groups, because teens relate best to other teens.

Help Is Available

Many times people who abuse drugs and alcohol are in denial that they have a problem. Even when confronted with the truth by a friend, it may be very difficult to face. But if a teen is abusing drugs, the best thing for him or her to do is to seek advice from a parent, doctor, teacher, guidance counselor, minister, rabbi, or other mentor. If this is not possible, many hot lines and Web sites are available (See the "Where to Find Help" section of this book.) No one needs to wrestle alone with abuse and addiction. Help is available.

What to Do If a Friend Has a Problem

If a teen thinks that a friend has a problem with drugs or alcohol, listening to that friend will help. Some young people turn to drugs because they are unhappy about a problem at school or at home. It may be very helpful for them to talk about a problem with an understanding friend.

It is important not to be judgmental with friends

who are in trouble. A person should not preach, for it will only make friends turn away. Instead, teens should voice their care and concern. They can offer to go with a friend to a support-group meeting or on a visit to a guidance counselor at school. They can give him or her educational materials about drug abuse. Any progress that a friend makes in confronting and fighting an addiction should be praised. Whenever a teen appears to be in serious trouble, a trusted adult—such as a parent, guidance counselor, or member of the clergy—must be consulted.

Where to Find Help

Al-Anon/Alateen Family Group Headquarters, Inc.
1600 Corporate Landing Parkway
Virginia Beach, VA 23454-5617
(888) 4AL-ONON
<http://www.al-anon.org>

Cocaine Anonymous World Services (CA)
P.O. Box 2000
Los Angeles, CA 90049-8000
(800) 347-8998

Marijuana Anonymous World Services
P.O. Box 2912
Van Nuys, CA 91404
(800) 766-6779
<http://www.marijuana-anonymous.org>

Narcotics Anonymous World Services (NA)
P.O. Box 9999
Van Nuys, CA 91409
(818) 773-9999
<http://www.na.org>

The National Center on Addiction and Substance Abuse at Columbia University (CASA)
Columbia University
152 West Fifty-Seventh Street, 12th Floor
New York, NY 10019-3310
(212) 841-5200
<http://www.casacolumbia.org>

National Clearinghouse for Alcohol and Drug Information (NCADI)
P.O. Box 2345
Rockville, MD 20847-2345
(800) 729-6686
<http://www.health.org>

National Council on Alcoholism and Drug Dependence (NCADD)
12 West Twenty-First Street
New York, NY 10010
(800) NCA-CALL
<http://www.ncadd.org>

National Directory of Drug Abuse and Alcoholism Treatment and Prevention Programs
<http://www.health.org/phone.htm>

National Inhalant Prevention Coalition
1201 West Sixth Street, Suite C-200
Austin, TX 78705
(800) 269-4237
<http://www.inhalants.com>

National Institute on Drug Abuse (NIDA)
National Institutes of Health
6001 Executive Blvd., Room 5213
Bethesda, MD 20892
(301) 443-1124
<http://www.nida.nih.gov>

Partnership for a Drug-Free America
405 Lexington Ave.
New York, NY 10174
(212) 922-1560
<http://www.drugfreeamerica.org>

Students Against Driving Drunk (SADD)
P.O. Box 800
Marlboro, MA 01752
(800) SADDINC
<http://www.saddonline.com>

Chapter Notes

Chapter 1. What Is Drug Abuse?

1. Michael Janofsky, "Fatal Crash Reveals Inhalants as Danger to Youth," *The New York Times*, March 2, 1999, p. A12.

2. National Council on Alcoholism and Drug Dependence, *Alcoholism Report*, vol. 26, No. 3, March 1998, p. 5.

3. Janofsky, p. A12.

4. National Institute on Drug Abuse (NIDA), "Monitoring the Future Study" conducted by the University of Michigan Institute for Social Research, 1998, <http://www.nida.nih.gov> (September 1999).

5. Patrick Perry, "Teen Drug Abuse: Bringing the Message Home," *The Saturday Evening Post*, May/June 1998, p. 16.

6. Ibid.

7. National Institute on Drug Abuse (NIDA).

8. Edward S. Traisman, ed., *American Medical Association Complete Guide to Your Children's Health* (New York: Random House, 1999), p. 196.

9. Ibid.

10. Herbert Kleber, *The Columbia University College of Physicians & Surgeons Complete Home Medical Guide*, 3rd ed., 1995, pp. 141–142.

11. Ibid.

12. Tamara K. Richards, "Abuse of Dextromethorphan-Based Cough Syrup as a Substitute for Licit and Illicit Drugs: A Theoretical Framework," *Adolescence*, Spring 1996, p. 239.

13. New York State Office of Alcoholism & Substance Abuse Services, "Questions & Answers About Drugs," pamphlet, n.d.

14. Ibid.

15. Ibid.

Chapter 2. Abuse of Legal Substances

1. The National Clearinghouse for Alcohol and Drug Information, <http://www.health.org> (September 1999).

2. Ibid.

3. Charles B. Clayman, ed., *The American Medical Association Family Medical Guide*, (New York: Random House, 1994), p. 27.

4. Mick Jagger and Keith Richards, *Rock On!*, vol. 2, *Illustrated Encyclopedia of Rock and Roll: The Modern Years, 1956 to Present*, ed. Norm Nited (New York: Thomas Crowell, 1978), p. 404.

5. Roger Granet, M.D., and Robin K. Levinson, *If You Think You Have Depression* (New York: Dell, 1998), p. 2.

6. Center for Substance Abuse Prevention, "Tips for Teens About Inhalants," brochure (New York: NYS Office of Alcoholism & Substance Abuse Services, 1997).

7. Jane E. Brody, "Dietary Supplements May Test Consumers' Health," *The New York Times*, September 22, 1998, p. F7.

8. Philip M. Boffey, "Post-Season Thoughts on McGwire's Pills," *The New York Times*, September 30, 1998, p. A16.

9. George Vecsey, "Mac Recalls a Different Kind of Race," *The New York Times*, August 21, 1999, p. D1.

10. "Ultimatum Is Given in Three Sports," *The New York Times*, November 28, 1998, p. D5.

11. *Facts About Alcohol and Other Drug Use Among Children and Teens* (Washington, D.C.: The American Council for Drug Education, n.d.), p. 1.

12. "Reports Show Drug Use Still a Problem Among U.S. Teenagers," *The Nation's Health* 27, No. 8, September 1997, p. 1.

13. Center for Substance Abuse Prevention, "Tips for Teens About Smoking," brochure (New York: NYS Office of Alcoholism & Substance Abuse Services, 1997).

14. Traisman, p. 199.

15. Center for Substance Abuse Prevention, "Tips for Teens About Smoking."

Chapter 3. Illegal Drugs

1. T. Trent Gegax and Sarah Van Boven, "Heroin High," *Newsweek*, February 1, 1999, p. 54.

2. National Institute on Drug Abuse (NIDA), "Monitoring the Future Study" conducted by the University of Michigan Institute for Social Research, 1998, <http://www.nida.nih.gov> (September 1999).

3. Ibid.

4. Kevin Flynn, "Arrests Soar in Crackdown on Marijuana," *The New York Times*, November 17, 1998, p. B1.

5. Center for Substance Abuse Prevention, "Tips for Teens About Crack and Cocaine," brochure (New York: NYS Office of Alcoholism & Substance Abuse Services, 1997).

6. Mark S. Gold, *800-Cocaine* (New York: Bantam Books, Inc., 1984), p. 5.

7. Timothy Egan, "A Drug Ran Its Course, Then Hid With Its Users," *The New York Times*, September 19, 1999, p. A1.

8. Seth Mydans, "Death of River Phoenix Is Linked to Use of Cocaine and Morphine," *The New York Times*, November 13, 1993, Section 1, p. 8.

9. Maureen Dowd, "Move Over Tootsie, It's Mrs. Doubtfire," *The New York Times*, November 21, 1993, Section 2, p. 1.

10. Mydans, p. 8.

11. Judy Monroe, "The LSD Story," *Current Health 2*, April/May 1998, p. 24.

12. Ibid.

13. Adam Gershenson, "For Homeless Youths in New York, A Search for Happy Endings," *The New York Times*, December 6, 1998, Section 1, p. 65.

14. William Chaze, "The Deadly Path of Today's PCP Epidemic," *U.S. News & World Report*, July 7, 1984, p. 65.

15. Erica Goode, "Nerve Damage Linked to Heavy Use of Ecstasy Drug," *The New York Times*, October 30, 1998, p. 27.

16. Senator John Kyl, "Guest Opinion," *Inside Tucson Business*, June 1, 1998, p. 5.

17. Thomas H. Maugh, II, "Amphetamine Use Soars in California, Study Finds," *The Los Angeles Times*, November 29, 1995, p. A1.

Chapter 4. Why Do Teens Do Drugs?

1. Edward S. Traisman, ed., *American Medical Association Complete Guide to Your Children's Health* (New York: Random House, 1999), p. 195.

2. Ibid., p. 475.

3. Charles B. Clayman, ed., *The American Medical Association Family Medical Guide* (New York: Random House, 1994), p. 762.

4. Traisman, p. 475.

5. Project Know, courtesy of U.S. Department of Education, "Growing Up Drug-Free: A Parent's Guide to Prevention," <http://www.onhealth.com> (1998).

Chapter 5. How to Get Help

1. Edward S. Traisman, ed., *American Medical Association Complete Guide to Your Children's Health* (New York: Random House, 1999), p. 196.

2. Center for Substance Abuse Prevention, *Keeping Youth Drug-Free* (U.S. Department of Health and Human Services: NCADI Publication No. (SMA)97-3194, 1997), p. 17.

3. Charles B. Clayman, ed., *The American Medical Association Family Medical Guide* (New York: Random House, 1994), p. 762.

4. David Van Biema, "Just Say Life Skills: A New School Antidrug Program Outstrips D.A.R.E.," *Time Magazine*, November 11, 1996, p. 70.

Cozic, Charles P. *Illegal Drugs*. San Diego, Calif.: Greenhaven Press, Inc., 1997.

Croft, Jennifer. *Drugs & the Legalization Debate*. New York: Rosen Publishing Group, 1997.

Grosshandler-Smith, Janet. *Drugs & the Law*, 2nd ed. New York: Rosen Publishing Group, 1997.

Kuhn, Cynthia. *Buzzed: The Straight Facts About the Most Used & Abused Drugs From Alcohol to Ecstasy*. New York: Norton, W.W., & Company, 1998.

Schleichert, Elizabeth. *Marijuana*. Springfield, N.J.: Enslow Publishers, 1996.

Washburne, Carolyn Kott. *Drug Abuse*. San Diego, Calif.: Lucent Books, 1996.

Weatherly, Myra. *Inhalants*. Springfield, N.J.: Enslow Publishers, 1996.

Winters, Paul A., ed. *Teen Addiction*. San Diego, Calif.: Greenhaven Press, 1997.

Index